# 1002 Questions on Life, Sex, and Relationships

JEBWizard Publishing
Books with Character

JEBWizard Publishing
Books with Character

# 1002 Questions on Life, Sex, and Relationships

By Susan Kardel

JEBWizard Publishing
Books with Character

# COPYRIGHT

Printed in the United States of America by IngramSpark

First Printing, July 2021

ISBN **Print: 978-1-7368288-0-9**

ISBN **ePub 978-1-7368288-1-6**

JEBWizard Publishing
37 Park Forest Rd,
Cranston, RI 02920
www.jebwizardpublishing.com

JEBWizard Publishing
Books with Character

# Dedication

This book is dedicated to my family and friends. If it weren't for you all pushing me, this wouldn't have happened. I LOVE YOU ALL Thank you very much!

# Table of Contents

# What is the Meaning of Life?

*"42"*

*A Hitchhiker's Guide to the Universe*
*by Douglas Adams*

Did you ever ponder the deep questions? Ever wonder at the universe, the stars, the Milky Way? Ever try to understand life and why it is the way it is?

If so, this book is not for you. This book poses practical questions we can ask ourselves, our friends, our significant others about life and what we want out of it.

Some are simple, some complex. Some require thought; some require little. Some require introspection, some just openness. Some may spark embarrassment, or reticence, or resistance.

Some of the questions are grouped by subject, others are just randomly arranged, all are designed to make you think about your life and the lives of those around you.

Thinking about your answers will show you how to better share this planet with those you love, those who love you, and those of whom you wonder how they ever made it this far in life.

There are no right answers, but there are answers right for you. Answers—if you look hard enough and face the truth—to living a good life.

Perhaps we should all live by this philosophy; *if you don't ask the question, the answer is always no.*

# Chapter One

1. What's a question you wish people would ask more often?

2. In what ways do we work well together?

3. What do you think is unpredictable? Why?

4. How much space/alone time should people in a relationship give each other?

5. If your mirror could speak, what would it say?

6. What could we do to strengthen our relationship?

7. What are you skeptical about? Why?

8. Complete this thought: I wish I had paid more attention <u>when</u>...?

9. Name something you wish was glow in the dark.

10. What do you think is worth waiting for?

11. What do you always have an excuse for?

12. What three words best describe our relationship?

13. How open-minded are you? If so, in what way?

14. Do you think "take it one day at a time" is excellent advice? Why or why not?

15. Do you feel you can talk to me about anything?

16. Do you believe everything happens for a reason, or do we just find reasons after things happen?

17. What gives you a sense of security?

18. What do you wish we could do more of?

19. What does love mean to you?

20. You mentor a troubled teen. What do you talk about that will make an impact in their life?

# Chapter Two

---

*"Plain question and plain answer
make the shortest road out of most
perplexities."* Mark Twain

---

**21.** When do I challenge you the most?

**22.** How have I improved your life?

**23.** If you could indulge in anything without consequence, what would it be?

**24.** What relationship or friendship do you regret ended?

**25.** Is there anything you need from me to continue growing as a person?

**26.** What strengths do I bring to our relationship?

**27.** Do you care about ethnicity? Why?

**28.** What are you looking forward to this week?

**29.** Do you think of yourself as a human being or a human doing?

**30.** How can I be a better spouse or partner to you?

**31.** What does the word "affection" mean to you?

32. If someone really wanted to understand you, what would they read, watch, and listen to?

33. What other ways can I better show you my appreciation?

34. Are you happy?

35. Is poverty in society inevitable?

36. What drains your energy in our relationship?

37. How do you measure success?

38. What is your definition of evil?

39. If you could say a sentence the entire world could hear, what would you say?

40. What is the difference between justice and revenge?

# Chapter Three

*"You can tell whether a man is clever by his answers. You can tell whether a man is wise by his questions."* Naguib Mahfouz

41. What is your pet peeve in a relationship?

42. What's on your mind right now?

43. What are you afraid to do?

44. Why are humans so confident in unproven beliefs?

45. How can I better support you?

46. How important to you is health-consciousness in a life partner?

47. How would you define genius?

48. Define yourself in one word.

49. How important is a sense of adventure to you in a life partner?

50. How do you define consciousness?

51. What traditions would you like to start this year?

52. Which is more important, what you say or the way you say it? Why?

53. How would the world look without money?

54. Does jealousy, as an emotion, have value?

55. How significant is wealth?

56. What is the biggest waste of human potential?

57. What answers are you searching for?

58. What two questions would you ask to get the most information about who a person truly is?

59. What's your biggest fear in our relationship?

60. What is your favorite conversation topic?

61. By what standards do you judge yourself?

62. Are there times when I am too critical?

63. What are your top three turn-ons?

64. How important is it for individuals in a relationship to maintain their own separate identities?

65. Is intelligence or wisdom more useful?

66. How has your love for me changed since marriage?

# Chapter Four

> *"Physics is like sex: sure, it may give some practical results, but that's not why we do it."*
> — *Richard P. Feynman*

67. What is your favorite sexual fantasy?

68. What type of sexual partner are you? Kinky, traditional, or bashful?

69. Which do you think is more important in a relationship, sexual or emotional compatibility?

70. What would you change about our sex life?

71. What is something you are sexually obsessed with?

72. What's the best way for me to start sex?

73. How sexually open-minded are you in a relationship?

74. Tell me a sexual fantasy you like; one you haven't told me yet?

75. My sexiest feature is?

76. What's your favorite sexual memory with me?

77. What's your favorite sex position?

78. What sex acts do you find off-limits or consider gross?

79. If we could have sex anywhere in public and not get caught, tell me where it would be.

80. Ask me anything you want to know about my sexual desire?

81. What is one of your sexual fantasies?

82. Rough sex or soft sex?

83. What's your kinky fetish?

84. Have you ever pretended to be the opposite sex? If not, would you want to Favorite sex position?

85. Sex on the bed, couch, or floor?

86. Do you prefer giving or receiving oral sex?

87. A song you'd listen to during hard/rough/kinky sex?

88. What is better than fantastic sex?

89. What is one place you would like us to have sex, but we have not?

90. A song you'd listen to during soft/slow passionate sex?

91. Are you into dressing up for sex?

92. Would you prefer sex in the bath or in the shower?

93. Have you ever had a threesome? If not, would you?

94. Early morning sex or late-night sex?

95. In what ways do you feel satisfied sexually?

96. What is your favorite body part of the opposite sex?

97. What is your favorite body part of the same sex?

98. What's one thing you really want to do sexually but have never done, and why?

99. What food would you like to use during a sexual experience?

100. Worst possible time to get horny?

101. Have/would you ever have sex in public?

102. Do you like oral sex? Why/why not?

103. When am I most sexy to you?

104. If you were the other sex for a day, what are five things you would do?

105. Which genital part of your body do you like being touched?

106. What is your sexual guilty pleasure?

107. What is the difference between sex and making love?

108. Would you rather be kinky or romantic?

109. Would you rather be choked while receiving pleasure or choke and slap someone while giving it to them?

110. How important do you think sex is in a relationship?

111. Are most of your friends the same sex or opposite sex?

112. What makes you uncomfortable when talking about sex?

113. What's your dirtiest sexual fantasy?

114. What is the most annoying thing about the opposite sex?

115. Would you ever have lesbian or gay sex?

116. What do you think the sexiest fruit is?

117. Where do you think would be the weirdest place to have sex? Would you have sex there?

118. What is something nonsexual that makes you horny?

**119.** Worst sexual idea you ever had?

# Chapter Five

---

*"An empowered life begins with serious personal questions about oneself. Those answers bare the seeds of success." Steve Maraboli*

---

**120.** What is your personality type?

**121.** What is something small we can do daily for each other to improve our lives?

**122.** Where does your self-worth come from?

**123.** How do you define love?

**124.** What stops people from understanding themselves?

**125.** What question do you most want an answer to?

**126.** What should be the goal of humanity?

**127.** What is the best part of our relationship/marriage?

**128.** Which is more important: The human body, or the human mind?

**129.** Do you trust me?

**130.** Does a person's name influence the person they become?

131. Do I show you enough respect?

132. When you erase a word with a pencil, where does it go?

133. What do you want out of life?

134. Does jealousy have value in driving humans to improve themselves, or is it a purely negative emotion?

135. What have you wanted to tell me but never found the courage to?

136. What brings meaning to your life?

137. When are you the most "you"?

138. If you had to become a part of a TV-stream which would you choose? Why?

139. Do you think the eyes are a window to a person's soul?

140. What makes you dislike a person?

141. If you had the resources to invent anything, what would it be?

142. What values are important to you?

143. What is the most annoying thing to you?

144. Would you rather fulfill your biggest wish or resolve your biggest regret?

**145.** If you could only shop at one store for the rest of your life, what would it be?

**146.** What is your definition of cheating?

**147.** What is one thing a woman/man should never do?

**148.** What kind of physical touch best says "I Love You" to you?

**149.** What is your idea of moral support?

**150.** What would you say are the aspects that draw you to me?

**151.** Do you believe in "an eye for an eye"?

**152.** What's the last decision you regretted?

**153.** Are you content with our relationship?

**154.** Are your needs being met in our marriage?

**155.** What would you like us to do that's adventurous?

**156.** What are the top 3 of your favorite things we do in bed?

**157.** What do you like about our intimacy?

**158.** What don't you like about our intimacy?

**159.** What do you value about me?

160. How do you think we should handle our disagreements differently?

161. Would you rather let your spouse date your best friend or your worst enemy?

162. What's your philosophy in life?

163. What's the most daring thing you've done?

164. What are the top three best things a boyfriend/girlfriend can do to make you feel special?

165. What outfits turn you on the most that women/men wear?

166. Would you rather lose all of your old memories or never be able to make new ones?

167. What was your first thought this morning when you woke up?

168. What matters to you the most in a relationship?

169. Name something kind or helpful that stands out to you that I have done for you?

170. If you were a bartender, what famous person would you like to serve?

171. What's your weirdest talent?

# Chapter Six

---

*"Never give up on someone.
Sometimes the answers you are
looking for are the same answers
another person is looking for. Two
people searching together are always
better than one person alone."*

— *Shannon L. Alder*

---

**172.** Your ideal hug would last how long?

**173.** In your opinion, what is the one thing we have argued about the most in the past 90 days? What do you think is the root cause, and how can we resolve it?

**174.** How would you describe our relationship in three words?

**175.** What is a question about life that you wish you had the answer to?

**176.** What are the top five things you appreciate about me?

**177.** Do you ask enough questions, or do you settle for what you know?

**178.** What is your current life mantra?

179. What message do you have for your spouse that you want her/him to always keep in mind?

180. Do you forgive and forget, just forgive but never forget or neither?

181. Do you influence people more than they influence you?

182. What makes you feel miserable?

183. Would you rather never get angry or never get envious?

184. What do "I" do that really turns you on?

185. How did you meet (spouse) and know she/he was the one?

186. If every person you killed made you live another ten years, how many people would you kill?

187. If I suggested something super kinky that freaked you out, would you try it anyway?

188. Something you fear might change you?

189. Are you an optimist, a pessimist, or a realist?

190. What is your most marked characteristic?

191. What did you wish your brain were better at doing?

192. What do you think I need most these last few days?

193. Where does a thought go when it's forgotten?

194. What is the purpose of setting goals if we all die anyway?

195. Why does anything exist?

196. If we need to follow rules at all costs, then why do we make exceptions to these rules?

197. What shape is your field of vision?

198. If killing people is wrong, then why do we kill people that kill people?

199. If you're trying to fail and you succeed, did you fail, or did you succeed?

200. What is the color of a mirror?

201. If you could change one thing about yourself, what would it be?

# Chapter Seven

---

*"We live in the world our questions create." David Cooperider*

---

**202.** Where have you gone and felt the most out of place?

**203.** What is your idea of perfect happiness?

**204.** Where is the line between art and not art?

**205.** What has made you cry or upset recently?

**206.** What is standing in your way right now?

**207.** If someone you loved was killed in front of you, but someone created a copy of them that was perfect right down to the atomic level, would they be the same person? Would you love them just as much?

**208.** How do you think we should show love?

**209.** Name one thing I do that makes you feel unloved?

**210.** What do you seek in a friend that you neither expect nor want in a lover?

211. Do you believe love has more to do with common interests, physical attraction, dependency needs, or timing and maturity level?

212. Is there anything you are ever a snob about?

213. Is free will real or just an illusion?

214. If you wrote a song about your love life, what would the title be?

215. What are some of the hard facts about life?

216. What harsh truth do you prefer to ignore?

217. Which element best represents you?

218. What's your next challenge?

219. What is the most annoying thing to you in a relationship?

220. How do you find fulfillment?

221. What is something you think everyone should experience in their lifetime?

222. What one thing makes our relationship better than other relationships?

223. What do I mean to you?

224. You must make room for...

225. What do you think I'd say is your most attractive quality?

226. One thing you're most concerned about?

227. Snakes: interesting or creepy? Why?

228. Your future in 3 words.

229. What kind of physical affection do you like?

230. If you woke up tomorrow and discovered that everything in life was now free, what is the first thing you would do?

231. What is something you've wished for repeatedly?

232. What are the 5 most important parts of a marriage? Rank them.

233. What's one secret you've wanted to tell me, but haven't?

234. On a scale of 1-10 how happy are you with life?

235. What expectations do you have of me as your spouse?

236. What's one thing you feel our relationship is lacking?

237. What takes too long?

238. What are you worried about?

239. Is there anything you need from me to continue growing as a person?

240. What traffic sign best reflects your life right now?

241. A song title that best describes your life?

242. Do you feel like I've helped you become a better person since marriage?

243. Do you believe there's one person you're "meant" to be with?

244. What are your biggest goals for the month?

245. What have you been able to accomplish this year that you are really proud of?

246. Is there something you stopped doing even though you loved it? Why'd you stop?

247. You are a children's book writer. Write the first few lines of your new book.

248. Who do you compare yourself to most?

249. Apart from Facebook, what do you like to do?

250. Are you afraid to speak your own opinion?

# Chapter Eight

**251.** What one job do you think computers/machines will never replace?

**252.** What do you believe stands between you and complete happiness?

**253.** What is increasingly becoming socially acceptable, but shouldn't be?

**254.** Best relationship advice you can give someone.

**255.** What would you like to ask yourself?

**256.** What is something we can only learn with age?

**257.** Do you feel accepted by me?

**258.** If you didn't have to sleep, what would you do with the extra time?

**259.** What's one thing in life that should always be free?

**260.** On a scale from 1 to 10, how happy are you with our marriage as it is right now? Why?

261. What is the biggest waste of time in your life?

262. How many dates would you like to go on each month to feel connected?

263. If you could be like one person, who would it be and why?

264. What skill do you wish more people took the time to learn?

265. Do you get enough alone time/time with friends?

266. Why are you worth knowing?

267. What's the most meaningful compliment you've ever received?

268. Do you feel like we understand each other more now?

269. What three events most shaped your life?

270. What are some of your greatest hopes?

271. What is more important, fear or hope?

272. If a genie gave you three wishes, what would they be? (A wish cannot be picked ☺)

273. What is your biggest day to day challenge?

274. Are you more worried about doing things right, or doing the right thing?

275. Do you prefer to be eaten or fingered?

276. Where do you go/what do you do when you need inspiration?

# Chapter Nine

---

*"Millions saw the apple fall, but Newton was the one who asked why."* Bernard M. Baruch

---

**277.** If you could only have one, spontaneity or stability, which one would you pick?

**278.** What has overwhelmed you lately?

**279.** What do you think about yourself?

**280.** If you could give your children one talent, what would it be?

**281.** Do you think you are not worthy of something that you have?

**282.** What accomplishments are you most proud of?

**283.** What do you usually think about on your commute home from work?

**284.** Do you feel at peace with me?

**285.** Do you have any unusual kinks/fetishes?

**286.** Would you ever sacrifice your being for a more significant cause?

**287.** What is your idea of fulfillment in life?

288. Do you have any collections? Why?

289. What is my most attractive quality?

290. What's something you love, but you don't understand why?

291. If you could master any skill, what would it be?

292. Is there anything I used to do for you wish I still did?

293. Is there anything I do that annoys you?

294. Do you like to be dominant or submissive?

295. Do you consider a threesome cheating?

296. If you were a color, what would you be and why?

297. If I allowed you to cheat on me with any 3 celebrities, what would it be?

298. If someone asked you to give an impromptu Ted talk, what would you talk about?

299. If you could choose to be immortal, would you?

# Chapter Ten

*It is not the answer that enlightens,
but the question- Eugene Jonesco*

**300.** What came as a surprise to you after we got married?

**301.** How can we communicate better?

**302.** How do you feel about supporting family members financially?

**303.** When someone offers you a penny for your thoughts, so you put your two cents in, where does the second penny go?

**304.** If you could lock one person in a room and torment them for a day, that person would be?

**305.** What have you learned to appreciate about me that you didn't know when we were first married?

**306.** What's challenging about being in a relationship?

**307.** Would you want to live a life that is free from challenges or obstacles?

**308.** Does life require a purpose?

**309.** What has made you laugh or brought you joy this week?

**310.** Would you rather break someone's heart or have your heart broken?

**311.** Are you satisfied with the way we share responsibilities? Explain why or why not?

**312.** Are you satisfied with the frequency and quality of our physical intimacy?

**313.** Where do thoughts come from?

**314.** If you could only keep one of your senses, what would it be?

**315.** The one thing that I couldn't have done without you was...

**316.** Is there anything you have always wanted to ask me, but didn't?

**317.** What else would you like to share with me?

**318.** What progress have we made towards the goals we set for this year? What things remain for us to do to achieve them?

**319.** Have you ever been on a blind date?

320. What's something you do the old-fashioned, non-tech way?

321. What makes a relationship healthy or unhealthy?

322. Was there something in the past or this week you need to forgive me for?

323. In what area of life do you most frequently feel as if you struggle to find healthy balance?

324. What are two things that refresh you, inspire you, and remind you of what's important to you?

325. The most annoying?

# Chapter Eleven

*Learn from yesterday, live for today, hope for tomorrow. The important thing is not to stop questioning. - Albert Einstein*

326. Shape shift or mind read? Would you prefer to control the physical or mental realm?

327. What is something that makes you excited when you're talking about it? When did you first become passionate about this topic?

328. What would you like to do more of in life, but don't? Why not?

329. If you do a good deed in order to feel good about it, is it kindness or business?

330. Where in your body do you feel emotion?

331. What do I do that turns you on the most?

332. Is there anything you feel insecure about in our relationship?

333. Something that will never fail to get you horny?

334. What is your primary focus?

335. What would you do if you were granted success?

336. If consciousness is a purely human trait, are we better off for it or does it simply lead to greater problems?

337. Can anything ever really be considered "true" or is everything subjective?

338. Who are you jealous of and why?

339. What do you value most in life?

340. What is your guilty pleasure?

341. What are you obsessed with?

342. In what ways do you feel satisfied with our relationship?

343. What is that one question you have always wanted to ask me but never asked?

344. What do you need help with?

345. What stops people from understanding themselves?

346. Name two people that remind you of yourself?

347. What do you appreciate about me?

348. What was the one thing that convinced you to marry me?

**349.** What do you dislike about yourself?

**350.** Is poverty an inevitable byproduct of human society?

# Chapter Twelve

*Too many people are trying to find the right person instead of being the right person. - Gloria Steinem*

**351.** What do you consider a wasted life?

**352.** How can we add more value to our quality time?

**353.** How can I be a better partner to you this week?

**354.** What offence do you consider unforgivable?

**355.** Tell me one thing I do that you utterly hate but have chosen to let go?

**356.** What is the difference between guilt and shame?

**357.** What does it mean to forgive?

**358.** Name a fantasy that I can fulfill for you, but you have never told me?

**359.** What does friendship mean to you?

**360.** What message would you like to share with your family?

**361.** What matters to you the most?

362. What is your favorite way to show your love to me?

363. What is the most valuable lesson you learned about your past relationship or our relationship?

364. What does the word "romance" mean to you?

365. How do you recharge?

366. What masks do you wear?

367. If your life were a book, what would the title be?

368. What is your most important need and desire in a relationship? Does your present life fulfill them?

369. How important is a sense of humor to you in a life partner?

370. Do you watch gay/lesbian porn?

371. Do you believe in heaven and hell?

372. Do you trust anyone in your life?

373. What is deeply unsettling?

374. Is human consciousness just electrons flowing through neurons, or is it something beyond physical?

375. What things remind you of me?

# Chapter Thirteen

---

*"Judge a man by his questions rather than by his answers." Francois Marie Arouet Voltaire*

---

**376.** What is one thing we can work on to be better partners?

**377.** Are you living a meaningful life?

**378.** What would you like us to do together that we've never done before?

**379.** If you had to sum up the whole human species in 3 words, what would those words be?

**380.** Where's your life headed?

**381.** Is there a memory or secret that I don't know about?

**382.** If you had to change one thing about me, what would you change?

**383.** Is there something you miss that we used to do?

**384.** Booty or boobs?

**385.** If you could give yourself head, would you?

**386.** When is your spouse at his/her best?

387. What is your purpose in life?

388. When someone says blood, you think...

389. What do you consider overrated in life?

390. When was the last time you felt taken care of?

391. When was the last time you felt like I didn't appreciate you?

392. What are 3 things on your bucket list?

393. Would you rather date someone you met online or go on a blind date?

394. If you could do it all over again, what would you change?

395. Notice the sensation in your body right now, what do you feel?

396. When you think about (spouse) how would you describe him/her?

397. When do you last remember laughing with me the most?

398. Do you like dirty talk?

399. What kind of porn do you like to watch?

400. They gave if you the opportunity to spend 48 hours with absolutely anyone (living or dead),

who would you spend it with and what would
you do?

# Chapter Fourteen

---

*"Asking questions is one of the fundamental keys of learning. It is always better to ask a question than pretend you understand." Catherine Pulsifer*

---

**401.**   What do you spend most of your money on?

**402.**   Who should take care of the elderly- the government, their families, or the elderly themselves?

**403.**   What does your inner critic tell you?

**404.**   Do you think morality exists in nature or is it a human construct?

**405.**   Why is depression so stigmatized in society?

**406.**   How important is confidence to you in a life partner?

**407.**   How important is punctuality to you in a life partner?

**408.**   Do you have trust issues?

**409.**   Do I stress you out?

**410.**   Do I fulfill all your needs physically?

411. Do you feel like I listen to you when you are speaking to me?

412. Would you choose to be immortal, if given the chance?

413. What did you love to do as a kid before high school?

414. Do you think we stay in love with some people forever?

415. Do you want to remain married?

416. Do you usually follow your head or your heart when making decisions?

417. What is something you are hesitant to tell me about my personality?

418. What is your favorite thing we do together?

419. What can I do to help strengthen our relationship?

420. What's one thing you hope happens in ~~the future~~ of our relationship?

421. What can I do to improve your life?

422. What chokes you up when you think about it?

423. What was the most awkward conversation you ever had with someone?

**424.** What is a controversial opinion that you have?

**425.** What fact do you try to ignore?

# Chapter Fifteen

*"I believe the qualities of our lives are determined by the people we meet, the books we read, and the questions we ask." David DeNotaris, Feeling Your Way Through Life*

426. What are the best and worst parts of human nature?

427. What is your favorite moment we've shared?

428. What is your favorite date we've had? Why?

429. When was the last time you felt loved?

430. What is one word that describes our relationship?

431. Describe each other in three words.

432. Are you happy (or satisfied) with your life at this moment?

433. Why do you love me?

434. How could I be a better partner to you?

435. How have we changed since we first started dating/married?

436. Where is your favorite place to escape to?

437. Is suffering an important part of being human?

438. Space exploration or ocean exploration?

439. Time or Space?

440. What is your weakness strength in our relationship?

441. What is your dream for us?

442. What is one thing you wish I did for you, but I don't?

443. What do you envy from other people's relationships?

444. What is your biggest strength in our relationship?

445. What mutual goal would you like to see us accomplish in the next 5 years?

446. What do I need to know most about you right now?

447. What have you learned to appreciate about me you did not know when we first got married?

448. What ways can I honor you more?

449. What are a few ways you deserve to see our finances improve?

450. What ways can I improve as a wife/husband?

# Chapter Sixteen

---

*Advice is what we ask for when we
already know the answer but wish we
didn't. – Erica Jong*

---

**451.** What part of my body would you want me to
tattoo?

**452.** What was the last thing you searched for on
your phone?

**453.** Would you rather be able to control fire or
water?

**454.** Would you rather live for a week in the past or
the future?

**455.** Is there anything I do that annoys you?

**456.** Do you feel like we understand each other more
now?

**457.** Are there times when I'm too critical?

**458.** If happiness were a currency, how rich would
you be?

**459.** If you could break any world record which one
would it be?

460. What is one thing you wish I would compliment you more on?

461. What have you learned about being married?

462. What can I do to make you feel more confident about us and our future?

463. Do your dreams have a deeper meaning?

464. What was the moment where you felt most motivated?

465. What are you holding onto that's holding you back?

466. What is the meaning of life? What is the meaning of your life?

467. What would you do if you restarted your life right now?

468. What could I do to make you feel more loved?

469. What could I do to make you feel more understood?

470. What can I do to make you feel more secure?

471. What could I do to make you feel more appreciated?

472. Do you have any big dreams that you have yet to share with me? And, if so, how can I help you achieve them?

473. What does honor mean to you?

474. What is the purpose of a human life?

475. What is the most interesting thing you heard this week?

# Chapter Seventeen

*Learn avidly. Question it repeatedly.
Analyze it carefully. Then put what
you have learned into practice
intelligently.* Confucius

**476.** What is the most memorable life advice you received?

**477.** What's the one thing you really want to do but have never done and why?

**478.** What do you like most about yourself?

**479.** What do you like least about yourself?

**480.** What are three healthy ways you can cope with anger?

**481.** What does being happy mean to you?

**482.** What spontaneous thing(s) have you done this month?

**483.** What is one thing that didn't work out in the past but you're so glad for it?

**484.** What two facts amaze you?

**485.** What is a challenge you would never want to face?

486. What is a topic that you feel you could feel lost in for hours?

487. What is the strangest thing you've done?

488. What story are you telling yourself right now?

489. Would you rather be able to change the future or the past; just by imaging it?

490. Would you rather die before your spouse or after?

491. Would you rather give up social media or eat the same dinner for the rest of your life?

492. Would you rather be married to someone good-looking who doesn't think you're attractive or be married to someone ugly who thinks you're gorgeous?

493. Have you ever been overly infatuated with someone?

494. If you had the attention of the world for just 10 seconds, what would you say?

495. Have you ever abandoned a creative idea that you believed in because others thought you were a fool? Explain.

**496.** Ten pleasant things about being in a relationship?

**497.** Ten challenging things about being in a relationship?

**498.** What is most important to you?

**499.** What are three things I need to stop doing?

**500.** What are three things I need to do more of?

# Chapter Eighteen

---

*"It is better to know some of the questions than all of the answers." James Thurber*

---

**501.** What is the one thing you learned this week?

**502.** What is a deal breaker in a relationship for you?

**503.** What do you feel your life is missing?

**504.** What steps are you taking to reach your goals?

**505.** What makes you upset?

**506.** What is your number 1 goal for next year?

**507.** Notice the thoughts that are passing by, what are they saying?

**508.** The most money you've bet on something?

**509.** Something about human anatomy you'd change?

**510.** How important is punctuality to you in a life partner? Scale 1-10.

**511.** How important is creativity to you in a life partner? Scale 1-10.

**512.** How important is physical beauty? Scale 1-10.

513. How important is spontaneity to you? Scale 1-10.

514. How important is ambition to you in a life partner? Scale 1-10?

515. How important is cleanliness to you in a life partner? Scale 1-10?

516. How important is fitness to you in a life partner? Scale 1-10?

517. How important is fitness to you? Scale 1-10?

518. How important is environmental awareness? Scale 1-10?

519. What do you think the hardest thing about marriage/being in a relationship is?

520. What are you into, but haven't told me about?

521. What are some things you really like about me?

522. What do you hope for?

523. Which band (current or past) would you want to go on tour with? (* Travel with, not perform)

524. Which makes you happier, to forgive someone or to hold a grudge? Explain.

525. Which member from any band would you want to lather in Nutella?

# Chapter Nineteen

*"If you don't ask,' why this?' often enough, somebody will ask 'why you?'" Tom Hirshfield*

**526.** What weird thing stresses you out more than it should?

**527.** What one thing are you worried will never change for you?

**528.** What gives you peace of mind?

**529.** What is something I did you thought was exceptionally kind or thoughtful?

**530.** What new hobbies or activities would you like to try together as a couple?

**531.** Would you rather ask permission or apologize later?

**532.** What could we do to strengthen our relationship?

**533.** Who is your favorite person?

**534.** Who has gotten you excited these days?

535. Who are you really? Who is behind the mask that you show to the rest of the world?

536. Who has been inspiring you lately?

537. Who could you ask?

538. Who do you trust the most in your life?

539. Who is your favorite relative from my side of the family?

540. Who do you seek most for advice?

541. What is the principal thing that influences your decisions?

542. What do you take for granted?

543. What is the saddest thing about your life that nobody knows?

544. What's your biggest regret?

545. What is one thing in life you can't decide on?

546. What's something that many people are afraid of, but you aren't?

547. What are you most sentimental about?

548. Tell me about a time you were heartbroken?

549. How do you express happiness?

550. How do you like to spend your free time?

# Chapter Twenty

*The people with charisma, those who attract others to themselves, are individuals who focus on others, not themselves. They ask questions of others. They listen. John C. Maxwell*

**551.** How do you feel about your relationship with your body?

**552.** How much personal time do you need each week to function well and feel happy?

**553.** How do you sabotage yourself?

**554.** How do you move past unpleasant thoughts and experiences?

**555.** How are you feeling at the moment?

**556.** How am I doing as a wife/husband in general?

**557.** How important is an outgoing personality in a life partner is to you? Scale 1-10.

**558.** How much attention do you require?

**559.** What life experiences did you miss out on?

**560.** What are your top 5 rules in life?

561. What prayer have you been praying for years and wonder if it will ever be answered?

562. What is something in your life you will never apologize for?

563. What does the word "success" mean to you?

564. What do you think about romance?

565. When do you feel closet to me?

566. When someone says calendars you think?

567. When is a good time to keep a secret?

568. Some people talk to figure out what they're thinking, and some people don't talk until they know what they're thinking. Which do you think I am? Which do you think you are?

569. If you knew you would die tomorrow, would you feel cheated today?

570. If you could ask yourself one question, what would it be?

571. If you were going on Dancing with the Stars, whom would you want as your partner?

572. Do you make time for what matters most to you?

573. Do you enjoy living alone or with someone?

**574.** One item you should throw away but probably never will

**575.** Name 3 things (or people) that make you smile.

# Chapter Twenty-one

> "Being religious means asking passionately the question of the meaning of our existence and being willing to receive answers, even if the answers hurt." Paul Tillich

**576.** Is what we perceive reality or just a construct of our minds? Can our minds correctly interpret reality or is reality subjective?

**577.** If you were guaranteed the correct answer to one question, what would you ask?

**578.** If you could be a bird which would you be?

**579.** If you could choose your last words, what would they be?

**580.** If you could have someone serenade you over a candlelight dinner, who would it be?

**581.** If you won a Nobel Peace Prize, what do you think it would be for?

**582.** What is legal that you think should be illegal?

**583.** What is the first impression you want to give people?

584. What profession do you think is the most undervalued today?

585. What have you ever run from that you needed to face?

586. What makes you unique?

587. What food best describes your personality?

588. What do you need to do to grow?

589. Are humans better at creation or destruction?

590. Are you holding onto to something that would be better to let go of? What is it and what's holding you back from letting go?

591. Are there any unresolved conflicts?

592. Are you more into looks or brains?

593. Are you a pacifist?

594. Are you more talk and less action or vice versa?

595. Describe yourself in terms of food?

596. How could you reinvent yourself?

597. How emotional are you?

598. How old do you think is too old to have a baby?

599. How long did you think our relationship would last when we first started dating?

**600.** How do you picture your life at 60?

# Chapter Twenty-two

---

*"Everything we know has its origins in questions. Questions, we might say, are the principal intellectual instruments available to human beings." Neil Postman*

---

**601.** How are you "Really"?

**602.** How important is it to you to be "in love"?

**603.** How often do you set goals for yourself?

**604.** How important do you think self-love is? Scale 1-10.

**605.** How do you feel about investing your money? Scale 1-10.

**606.** How judgmental are you towards other people?

**607.** How much affection do you need to feel happy?

**608.** What personality trait in people raises a red flag with you?

**609.** What is your motto?

**610.** What gives you cheap thrills?

**611.** What is your favorite occupation?

**612.** What is your most treasured possession?

**613.** Which historical figure do you most like to have a conversation with?

**614.** Which talent would you most like to have?

**615.** What event would you rather die than live through?

**616.** One word that best describes you?

**617.** What do you consider underrated in life?

**618.** What do you most dislike about your appearance?

**619.** What is the quality you most like in a man?

**620.** What is the quality you most like in a woman?

**621.** What would you like said about you at your funeral?

**622.** What is a priority for you right now?

**623.** What do you want more out of life? Happiness or success?

**624.** What do you think you are designed for in this life?

**625.** What is a personality trait that you admire in other people?

# Chapter Twenty-three

*"You don't have to answer every question that comes to your mind because some questions are like matryoshka dolls; once opened, new ones come out!" Mehmet Murat Ildan*

**626.** What is the worst emotion a human being can feel?

**627.** What requires your patience today?

**628.** If you could change one personality trait about yourself, would you? Which one?

**629.** If you had a pet parrot, what would you teach it to say?

**630.** If you had a 'do-over' button, what one event in your life would you like to have a second chance at?

**631.** If I said you could date other people, would you?

**632.** If our relationship ended, what's the one thing about it you'd miss the most?

**633.** If something happened where I had to move very far away, would you attempt long distance? Or go our separate ways?

**634.** If you were a book, in what section of the book shop would you be in?

**635.** If you had one word to describe our relationship what would it be?

**636.** What is the most useful tool you own?

**637.** What do you need the most to heal?

**638.** What wild things would you love to try?

**639.** What would you truly regret not doing if you died tonight?

**640.** What emotion do you have to prioritize?

**641.** What does this relationship mean to you?

**642.** What has made you angry this week?

**643.** What's one thing I do that makes you feel good that you wish I did more?

**644.** What's one thing about life you would never change for someone else, including me?

**645.** What's one thing you hope happens in the future of our relationship?

**646.** Do you trust yourself?

647. Do you feel comfortable expressing yourself?

648. Do you feel valued?

649. Do you have an image of something you'll never forget? To tell or not to tell?

650. Do you believe there's any scientific evidence supporting astrology?

# Chapter Twenty-four

---

*"Seeking answers to questions is what draws us forward. When you have no more questions you live in the satisfaction of the present moment. You have no more questions when you finally learn that love is the answer. Love is always the answer."*
*Kate McGahan*

---

**651.** Do you trust me completely?

**652.** Do you think it's more important to love or be loved?

**653.** Do you trust people that don't look you in the eye?

**654.** Do you like to revive bad news sugar coated or bluntly?

**655.** Do you believe confession is good for the soul?

**656.** Tell me about a time you had to let go of something you loved or wanted?

**657.** Complete this thought: "I would never..."

**658.** Do you think there's such a thing as the 'right' person for you?

659. Do you think I'm the "right" person for you? (If yes) What about me makes me the right person?

660. Do you prefer taking risks or having a safety net?

661. Do you like kissing or hugging more?

662. Do you believe that I love you?

663. Do you believe the way we dress affects how we think?

664. Do you have trust issues?

665. Do you think it's okay to hurt someone you love in order to protect them?

666. Do you believe material possessions can bring you happiness?

667. Do you live to work or work to live?

668. What would you do if you were invisible?

669. What keeps you awake at night?

670. What drains your energy?

671. What advice would you tell your 25-year-old self?

672. What three words describes you best?

**673.** What do you think is the most important question in life?

**674.** In what way are you selfish?

**675.** When have you experienced "heaven on earth"?

# Chapter Twenty-five

**676.** Are there any lines that you simply will not cross?

**677.** Tell me a time you said "NO".

**678.** Can you still be in love with someone and not be with them?

**679.** Think about the various roles you play in your life, if you had to give up all but one; Which one would you keep?

**680.** Complete this thought: "Someone, really needs to design a better..."

**681.** What about our relationship makes you really happy?

**682.** What's one difference between us you absolutely love?

**683.** What's one similarity between us that you absolutely love?

684.   What about me made you fall in love?

685.   What do you need to let go of?

686.   If someone gave $100, what would you spend it on?

687.   What is the biggest trigger for stress in your life?

688.   What is something you would still buy if it cost twice as much as it cost today?

689.   What do you need right now?

690.   What do you think is the most important thing for today's kids to learn in school?

691.   What stupid question have you heard someone ask (or asked yourself)?

692.   What color do you feel like today?

693.   What do you remember most about your teenage years?

694.   What is one mistake that you will never do again?

695.   What's something that no one else knows about you?

696.   What's one thing you wish to accomplish before you die?

697.   Tell me how your life might be 10 years in the future?

698.   What are you really lazy about?

699.   What do you look forward to every week?

700.   What are you addicted to?

# Chapter Twenty-six

*"The only way to learn new things is to ask questions and be curious. Find the people who inspire your curiosity because those are the ones you will learn from the most." James Altucher*

**701.** What is difficult about being married to me?

**702.** What chapters would you separate your autobiography into?

**703.** If you were to remain single for the rest of your life do you think you could be happy?

**704.** What is one thing you NEVER want me to change about myself?

**705.** Which world culture is the most fascinating to you?

**706.** Can a person fall in love with two people at the same time?

**707.** What are you experiencing?

**708.** What is reality?

**709.** What is the biggest "What if" that you are holding onto?

**710.** Would you rather drink a pint of your enemy's urine while they look you in the eye or eat a bowl of you own feces while everyone you've ever dated watches?

**711.** Would you rather slice your eye in half with a razor blade or swallow 10 needles?

**712.** You meet your 15-year-old self, you're allowed to say 3 words. What do you say?

**713.** If you could invite 3 people to dinner, who would they be?

**714.** If I went missing, my body never recovered, would you move on or devote your life to looking for me? If you did move on, how long would you wait?

**715.** If a crystal ball could tell you the truth about your life, me, or the future, what would you want to know?

**716.** What do you look for most in a spouse?

**717.** What do you think about doing a good deed for the sake of a reward? Do you think it diminishes the goodness of the deed?

718. If you could get wasted with a famous person who would that be?

719. If you could listen to only one song for the rest of your life, what would it be?

720. What have you been interested in or learning about lately?

721. What celebrity do you idolize the most?

722. What do you need less of?

723. What is your spouse's most difficult challenge?

724. How long are you willing to work on our marriage?

725. What is something you comprised on in a relationship that you wish you hadn't?

# Chapter Twenty-seven

**726.** What do you try to keep an open mind about?

**727.** Would you rather I be good in the kitchen or good in the bedroom?

**728.** Does Time have a beginning or end?

**729.** Do the needs of the many outweigh the needs of the few?

**730.** How do you explain consciousness?

**731.** What is truth?

**732.** Is suicide justifiable?

**733.** How do you know you're not dreaming right now?

**734.** What is a person? Is it the mind, or the body?

**735.** If voting is personal... why do people get mad at other people for voting for their self-interest?

**736.** Have you had to sacrifice things to be with me?

**737.** What else would you like to share with me?

738. What is your favorite thing about being married?

739. Is there something annoying I do that I need to be mindful of stop doing?

740. What if you could keep one memory of us together?

741. When is communication essential?

742. How well do you think we communicate?

743. How jealous are you when it comes to your significant other?

744. Is it better to trust people or not trust people? And why?

745. What do you think is the biggest violation of privacy?

746. If you could live one day over and over again for the rest of your life, which day would it be?

747. What is your biggest fear in life?

748. What is the one thing you wish I did differently as a Mom/Dad?

749. What has required you to put constant thought into?

**750.** Would you rather be with someone feared or loved by all?

# Chapter Twenty-eight

---

*"The master key of knowledge is, indeed, persistent and frequent questioning." Peter Abelard*

---

**751.** Would you ever take back someone who cheated?

**752.** Has someone ever given you a "last chance" and for what?

**753.** How would you like to die?

**754.** When was the last time someone truly listened to you?

**755.** Which is stronger-love or hate?

**756.** What is the strangest thing you have in your room? (you are not allowed to explain why you own it?)

**757.** Tell me about the middle of anything?

**758.** What's your favorite way to show affection?

**759.** Complete this thought... I wish an alarm would notify me whenever...

**760.** At what point are we good enough? When are we self-improved enough to accept ourselves?

**761.** What are you looking forward to in the coming months?

**762.** What are you most likely very wrong about?

**763.** What keeps you going every day?

**764.** What does it really mean to love someone?

**765.** When you look into the past, what do you miss the most?

**766.** What is a failure for you?

**767.** What's the most irrational thought that you have ever had?

**768.** In your opinion, what is the one thing we have argued about the most in the past 90 days?

**769.** What is your biggest source of disappointment?

**770.** What is something you really want to do in life that you haven't experienced yet?

**771.** What have you learned from your biggest mistake?

**772.** What is that one thing in your life you will not trade for anything?

**773.** What is your favorite thing about me?

774. What makes you feel empowered?

775. What is something you wish your spouse did better?

# Chapter Twenty-nine

---

*"Better to ask a question than to remain ignorant." Proverbs*

---

**776.** What three events most shaped your life?

**777.** Is there anything you feel you can't trust me with?

**778.** Is there anything that happened between us in the past that still bothers you?

**779.** What do you want us to improve on?

**780.** What do you feel your needs are in our marriage?

**781.** What do you believe love has more to do with: -common interests, -physical attraction, -dependency needs, timing, or maturity level?

**782.** How often do you reevaluate your life?

**783.** If there was a horrible accident and you were unconscious and on life support, how long would you want to be on life support?

**784.** Has anyone ever said, "I love you" and you couldn't say it back?

785. If you had a friend who spoke to you the same way you speak to yourself, would you keep them as a friend?

786. What disease are you most fearful of contracting?

787. What's one time lately that I've made you feel great about yourself?

788. What are you superstitious about?

789. Who influenced your life the most?

790. Something on your "to do" list that never gets done

791. What inspires your ideas?

792. What type of person angers you the most?

793. When and where were you the happiest?

794. You have a child and you have written one piece of advice that will be carried in his/her pocket for life, what is that advice?

795. What were the three best decisions of your life?

796. What's one quality about me that I see as a flaw that you absolutely love?

797. What is something in your life that is "worth it"?

**798.** Is there something I can do to make being married to me easier?

**799.** What comes to mind when you think about growing up in your hometown?

**800.** If you had to sum up human nature in 3 words, which would you choose?

# Chapter Thirty

---

*"At the end of the day, the questions
we ask of ourselves determine the
type of people that we will become."*
*Leo Babauta*

---

**801.** What is the ideal life?

**802.** What is the dumbest idea that you have ever had?

**803.** What would you do if I changed my religious beliefs?

**804.** What do you need more of?

**805.** Is there anything I do that brings you down?

**806.** Would you say our relationship has been mostly good, mostly bad, or somewhere in between?

**807.** Describe yourself in 3 musicians

**808.** What if I got really fat?

**809.** What are three things you can't live without?

**810.** Use one word to describe your confidence level?

**811.** A memory you think of often?

812. What is a wish you make again and again?

813. Would you break the law to save a loved one?

814. Do you owe me an apology for anything?

815. What's the weirdest thing you can do with Jell-O?

816. What is my grossest habit and how does it make you feel?

817. Who/what do you consider visionary?

818. Do you think ignorance is bliss?

819. What makes you lose sleep?

820. Have you ever resented someone, if so what for?

821. If you were to die and come back as a person or a thing, what would it be?

822. What is strength?

823. Where is your favorite place to be with me?

824. Name one thing you have lied to yourself about, why did you do this?

# Chapter Thirty-one

---

*"One common thing about great achievers is that they keep asking useful questions every day. They ask questions like; What do I want and what do I need to do to get it?"*
*Israelmore Ayivor*

---

825. If you could only keep 5 of your Facebook/Instagram/or Tic/Toc friends, who would they be?

826. If you could be a spice what would it be?

827. What would you compare our relationship to?

828. What could you give a 40-minute presentation on with absolutely no preparation?

829. What do you do repeatedly that you hate doing?

830. What inner demons keep you up at night?

831. If you were to make a biopic on your life, who would you cast as yourself?

832. When do you feel respected by me?

833. Tell me about somewhere you've been that you would like to go back to?

834. What do you never get tired of and why?

835. What is one of the most interesting things you learned about me?

836. I need some advice. Not about anything in particular. Give me random advice.

837. Who's the last new friend you made?

838. What could you redo? Should you?

839. What no longer serves you?

840. What do you miss when you give in to a fear of missing out?

841. What's your philosophy in life?

842. What is something that scares you about yourself?

843. What's one manipulative behavior of mine which pisses you off?

844. On a scale of 1 to 10. How important is confidence to you in a life partner?

845. Can you honestly say you're enjoying your life right now?

846. What happens when you give something your full attention?

847. What will you reach by slowing down?

# Chapter Thirty-two

*"I never learn anything by talking. I only learn things when I ask questions." Lou Holtz*

848. What lesson do you keep learning and re-learning?

849. Something is just beginning. What is it?

850. What would you take if you had to leave tonight?

851. What do you feel connected to?

852. When you find someone physically attractive, what's the first thing you notice?

853. Would you rather lose all of your money and valuables or lose all the pictures you have ever taken?

854. If you could be trained in any one thing by top professionals, what would you choose?

855. If this week had a theme to it, what would yours be?

856. What needs to change?

857. In this moment, are you okay?

858. What are you searching for?

859. What did you almost not notice about today?

860. Are you open to change?

861. What's your favorite non-physical quality about me?

862. What will you never give up on?

863. What do you love the most?

864. Think of a couple you greatly respect. What are three things you admire about their relationship?

865. What would you change about the way you were raised?

866. What do you wish someone would say to you?

867. What are you afraid might happen?

868. How was your day?

869. Long ago you planted a seed. What was it?

870. Do you have enough?

871. Three words better than I Love You?

872. What's one question you hate being asked?

# Chapter Thirty-three

---

*"A prudent question is one-half
of wisdom." Francis Bacon*

---

**873.** What do you feel are the biggest stressors in our marriage?

**874.** What helps you keep things in perspective?

**875.** Where is your center?

**876.** Can you close your eyes and take a deep breathe? What happens when you do?

**877.** Can you reframe a current problem as an opportunity?

**878.** Is there a truth that could set you free?

**879.** What is so simple you often forget about it?

**880.** What minor pleasures do you enjoy the most?

**881.** Would you rather try something new or create something new?

**882.** What makes you feel unattractive?

**883.** What nasty habit would you like to change?

**884.** When was the last time you felt guilty?

**885.** What memory makes you smile?

886. What is exactly right about this moment?

887. What does it mean to have inner peace?

888. What do you promise yourself?

889. What have you known from the start?

890. When have you give up on something?

891. What is something or someone that makes you the most vulnerable?

892. What are one or two things you have done this week that you've really enjoyed?

893. What legacy would you like to leave behind?

894. What can you say about solitude?

895. What problem doesn't seem to have an answer right now?

896. What would you want someone to do with this journal after you die?

897. What is something you do more out of obligation than enjoyment?

898. What are you curious about?

# Chapter Thirty-four

899. What do you think are the 5 most beautiful things on earth? Why?

900. How forgiving are you?

901. Do you protect empty days on the calendar?

902. Is there some irritating advice that might actually help you?

903. Who might be helping you by not helping you?

904. What would you put on your vision board?

905. What are you hiding?

906. Have you tried to understand your shadow?

907. What are you wondering?

908. What is unchanging?

909. Do you know yourself?

910. Where is your heart?

911. What do you think about the statement "Things happen for a reason"?

912. What lasts forever?

913. If you were given three things to make you happy, what would these be?

914. Does an answer count as an answer if it's another question?

915. What makes you, you?

916. What is the truth?

917. What is reality?

918. Why do people fear losing things they do not even have yet?

919. Is trust more important than love?

920. Where does the soul live?

921. What are numbers?

922. Is mind or matter more real?

923. Anything you want more of? Less of?

924. Is there anything you'd like to discuss?

925. What do you find difficult to discuss with me?

926. What are you feeling about you and me?

927. What feelings are you scared of expressing?

# Chapter Thirty-five

*"The key to wisdom is this—constant and frequent questioning, for by doubting we are led to question, by questioning we arrive at the truth."*
Peter Abelard

**928.** If you came with a warning label, what would it say?

**929.** If you could know one thing about your future, what would it be?

**930.** What's something you're glad you'll never have to do again?

**931.** What should a healthy relationship provide for the people in it?

**932.** Do you believe everything happens for a reason, or do we just find reasons after things happens?

**933.** If you could pick one of your life to do-over, which would it be and why?

**934.** What is one behavior that you never tolerate?

**935.** What is something that never ends well?

**936.** What about our relationship makes you really happy?

**937.** If you had one word to describe our relationship what would it be?

**938.** What's your biggest fear for this relationship?

**939.** What's one difference between us you absolutely love?

**940.** How should I communicate a problem or a concern to you?

**941.** What are your deepest emotional needs?

**942.** What words should I never say to you even in playfulness?

**943.** What could I do that would cause you to pull away from me?

**944.** What habits do I have that are upsetting to you?

**945.** What do you expect from me you should really be expecting of yourself?

**946.** What need of yours have I not been able to satisfy?

**947.** What should a healthy relationship look like?

**948.** Is our current relationship working?

**949.** How does being in love affect your life?

**950.** What are you grateful for about our relationship?

# Chapter Thirty-six

*"Our lives are shaped by the questions we ask. Good questions lead to good outcomes. Bad questions lead to bad outcomes." Michael Hyatt*

951. What's the toughest decision you made today?

952. What's the toughest decision you made this year?

953. What have you forgotten?

954. What's it like being you right now?

955. What's the most beautiful word in the world?

956. What makes you laugh more than anyone?

957. What did your father teach you?

958. What did your mother teach you?

959. How many times a day do you look in the mirror?

960. What activity do you do that makes you feel most like yourself?

961. What makes you feel supported?

962. What makes you feel safe?

963. What's the coolest thing about science?

964. What bad habit do you have?

965. Whom are you envious of?

966. When did you know?

967. What can you do better?

968. When are you most yourself?

969. What superpower would you most like to have?

970. If you were granted three wishes, what would you do with the second wish?

971. What is your actual superpower?

972. What's the best sound in the world?

973. What's perfect about your life?

974. How many times a day do you think about money?

975. What's one thing you're certain of?

976. What makes you cringe?

977. What crime have you considered committing?

# Chapter Thirty-seven

---

*"A wise man never regrets the questions he asks. Only the ones he didn't ask." Ted Bell*

---

**978.** If you could give one piece of advice to pass on to the next generation, what would it be?

**979.** If you learn from anyone in the world, who would you like to learn from?

**980.** What are you exceptional at?

**981.** If you could tell someone something anonymously what would it be?

**982.** What are you ashamed of?

**983.** What are you not saying right now?

**984.** What do you used to cope when you're feeling uncomfortable?

**985.** What makes you feel unstoppable?

**986.** How do you see me?

**987.** What emotion do you experience the most?

**988.** Do you think you're brave?

**989.** Is it easy for you to show yourself love or speak kindly to yourself?

**990.** What makes you feel super loved?

**991.** Are you more afraid of death or not really living?

**992.** What do you think makes you smile?

**993.** What scares you the most?

**994.** What is more important to you-status, power, or money?

**995.** Is there anything you see inside of yourself you're not sure of?

**996.** Would you be with someone who doesn't have the same beliefs as you?

**997.** Do you think confessions make a relationship stronger?

**998.** What's the one thing that people always misunderstand about you?

**999.** Would you say that I understand what you are feeling?

**1000.** Which famous TV family would you fit in perfectly?

**1001.** If you could pick my profession for me based on what you think I'm meant to do, what would it be?

**1002.** Would you lie to make me happy and where would you draw the line?

# About the Author

Susan Kardel, born and raised in East Providence, RI, now lives in Swansea, Mass.

A mother of two, Ashlee and Nathan, she has been in the medical field for over 25+ years. She is a coffee addict.

Sue loves spending time with her kids, listening to music, photography, journaling, fitness, cooking, and spending time outdoors. She is one who will drop what she is doing to help you if you need a helping hand.

This is a book for personal growth, a tool for deepening relationships, a lively conversation starter for family or friends. It poses over 1,000 questions that invite people to explore the most fascinating of subjects—themselves—and how they really feel about life, the world, and their place in it.

# About JEBWizard Publishing

**JEBWizard Publishing** offers a hybrid approach to publishing. By taking a vested interest in the success of your book, we put our reputation on the line to create and market a quality publication. We offer a customized solution based on your individual project needs.

Our catalog of authors spans the spectrum of fiction, non-fiction, Young Adult, True Crime, Self-help, and Children's books.

Contact us for submission guidelines at

https://www.jebwizardpublishing.com

Info@jebwizardpublishing.com

Or in writing at

**JEBWizard Publishing**
**37 Park Forest Rd.**
**Cranston, RI 02920**

CPSIA information can be obtained
at www.ICGtesting.com
Printed in the USA
BVHW030442150922
646968BV00007B/95